The Father's Love
Journey of a Soul

A message to our youth and a guide for Catholics, ex-Catholics, aspiring Catholics or Christians wanting to know more about Catholics or go deeper into their Christian roots.

By Jose L. Anaya

First edition–2002

© 2002 by José L. Anaya

Cover design by Magdalena L. Ubertini
Text edited by Magdalena L. Ubertini and Kristy Meyer

Inquiries and additional orders to:
     Jose L Anaya
     P.O. Box 114
     Carmel, IN 46082
     Email: jose0404@aol.com

Scripture quotations are from the Catholic Living Bible.

ISBN: 0-9718127-0-5

Table of Contents

Preface

Our personal road to salvation was made possible about 2,000 years ago through the death and resurrection of the sacrificial lamb, Jesus Christ. My family's road to salvation was smoothed over or facilitated by the faith and obedience of my ancestors.

In the summer of 1999, my three younger daughters and I went on a trip through Mexico so they could see a bit of their heritage and learn something about the culture. But, in reality I was the one that received more than I could have ever dreamed possible from that two-week journey. While visiting a second cousin she gave me a cassette and a newspaper article to give to my mother with whom she had grown up with near Guadalajara.

That article had a story of a Christian conflict that took place in Mexico during their early childhood. I have since found out more about this Cristero Rebellion of 1927–1929. In Mexico, articles were drawn up to their Constitution in 1917 outlawing monastic order, forbidding public worship outside the confines of churches, placing restrictions on the right of religious organizations to hold property, depriving clergy members of basic rights, making them, in effect, second-class citizens. Priests and nuns were denied the right to wear clerical attire, to vote, to criticize government officials or to comment on public affairs in religious periodicals. All these laws were on the books and made life uneasy for the religious although they were not initially strictly enforced. All this came to an end when a new leader, President Calles took office in 1926, a fanatic bent on exterminating Catholicism in Mexico. Not only did he enforce the constitution provisions, but added more of his own anti-Catholic legislation. The cassette contained stories of some of the men, women and priest among the catholic organizations that raised arms in resistance to a government that was attempting to destroy them.

Among that group of men was my great-grandfather, Gavino Flores, who led a band of Cristeros (Christians) in the Guadalajara area against the federal forces that were sent to enforce the laws of their new leader. Ultimately, my great grandfather was killed along with a brother and one of his sons. Others, including my grandfather and an uncle, were incarcerated but later released when the ransom, I mean bail, was paid in "their weight in gold and silver." My great-grandfather was a wealthy rancher and he gave up his land, cattle, money and ultimately his life for his faith.

Funny how all the Americanized articles I could locate on this subject depicts the faithful citizenry as religious fanatics or fanatical Catholics.

This information was nice to know and it made me proud and maybe a little boastful but it stayed in the back of my mind for about a year until I started reading Hebrews. In Hebrews 7:9-10, "for although Levi wasn't born yet, the seed from which he came was in Abraham when Abraham paid the tithes to Melchizedek." All of sudden a light went on in my head and I started thinking about David and the promises made to him and his ancestors for their faithfulness to God. His own son Solomon who had more wisdom than anyone at the time and more money than anyone in that known world still turned his back on God, but God remained faithful

3

because of his Word to David. Then, I flashed back to Abraham and the promises made to him for his faithfulness. His son Isaac was protected and saved and so was Jacob because of the promises to Abraham, and he was able to fulfill his destiny.

What is it that kept him on course to fulfill his destiny? What kept me from doing harm to myself and others by my foolish acts and behavior as a youth? What saved my family, some 30 years ago, when traveling at about 70 mph we experienced a blowout that sent our station wagon spinning and falling down a deep ravine, but landing safely down below in an upright position? Other motorists that stopped to see if we were all right could not believe our vehicle did not flip over as we went down that ravine. I had read the answer days earlier but did not understand it's full meaning until now. In Hebrews 1:14 it says, "for the angels are only spirit-messengers sent out to help and care for those who are to receive his salvation." Could it be that the same promises made to Abraham and David were also made to my great-grandfather for his faithfulness? I would like to think so since our God's promises and Word are the same yesterday, today and forever (also found in Hebrews). The Lord gives his promise and he faithfully fulfills it. He moves regardless of how good or holy we are, or even how obedient we are. He seems to say, "I make this promise, not because you deserve it, but this is how I desire to work in this area." He is sovereign.

Many books have been written on the topic of healing of one's family tree, of generational healing that may need to take place in order to heal oneself. This is good and it is a necessary action to complete one's healing process. To date, I have not seen any books written on the topic of starting *new* roots in the family tree. While we need to have that generational healing from something our ancestors have done, we can smooth the path for our descendants. Instead of being satisfied with being one of the branches, we can get into the root system and go deep to strengthen, feed and support the family tree facilitating the growth of others. If we are faithful to God, just as Abraham and David were, he will bless our seed for generations to come.

On the last night of the trip to Mexico with my daughters, I thought it would be nice to visit with a cousin I grew up with in Chicago who had moved to Mexico about 17 years earlier. She sensed uneasiness in me and asked where my wife was. I had to tell her of my year-long separation and further tales of woe. She listened and then started speaking of Jesus and how he loved me and could comfort me. Then she went on to try to explain a revival going on in the church; a charismatic revival that I should look into when I got back home. She also supplied me with a list of books to read. I told her I had started going to a Christian Church, and she challenged me as to what I knew about the catechism of the Catholic Church. Then her husband, whom I had known to be a very quiet and shy person, spoke to me about how his life was turned around. He was giving retreats twice a month and filling up churches with the same conviction and passion she had. It left me wondering what was going on?

Upon my return home I located a few of the books she suggested along with others about a healing ministry and salvation. Curious to see this first hand, I contacted my local church and the diocesan office in Indianapolis but received no answers. I went to the library and on the Internet found information on the charismatic movement and healing masses that were going on in Lafayette, Indiana and in Cincinnati, Ohio. I made the trip to Cincinnati and in my naivete and in anticipation of the huge crowds of people I had read about in other countries, I arrived three hours early to make sure I would get a seat inside the church. Only about 20–30 people showed for mass that evening and to make matters worse, they seemed to be all foreigners praying in funny languages which I was not familiar with. After mass, the priest made himself available for confession and two groups of people gathered at the altar to pray for others. Confession seemed like a good place to start since I hadn't been in some 25 years. Towards the end of confession I braced myself for what I knew was going to be a long, hard penance. I would probably be saying the Rosary from now until the end of the year. Instead, the priest told me the story of the prodigal son and gave me one Hail Mary to say. What a shock and a relief that was. I was anxious to leave knowing he had made some mistake. Now, I have never been exposed to this idea of personal prayer before, but since I had made the two-hour drive, went on to get prayed with. The woman gave me a Word of knowledge that left me wondering how she could possibly know things about me since she had never seen me before.

We then exchanged phone numbers and they later called me and gave me the name of a friend in Indianapolis affiliated with Presentation Ministries. They in turn led me to the prayer group in Carmel. I had traveled 3,000 miles from home to find, not necessarily what I was looking for but what I needed in my own backyard! From there, I attended a Life in the Spirit Seminar and later a Charismatic Retreat where I received the Baptism of the Holy Spirit.

Ironically, I had traveled to the same town where my great-grandfather had given his life decades earlier for our God.

Just before receiving the Baptism of the Holy Spirit, I was filled with confusing thoughts about most areas in my life. This same confusion and cloudy thinking, which causes us to ridicule, mock, make light of that which we do not understand.

I didn't understand my religion that well, but had just enough religion to hate the people making wars, abortionists and homosexuals, and all that they stood for. But now, while I don't condone or support their lifestyle of unnatural, immoral and un-Godly behavior, I don't hate them anymore. Now I look for scriptural guidance and find this guidance on homosexuality in the Old Testament book of Leviticus, as well as in Romans in the New Testament. If the homosexuals think they are being picked on or restricted, they should look at the list of don'ts that heterosexuals have to live with in Leviticus.

I was being swayed into accepting abortion under certain circumstance or for these reasons. Now I see life as a gift from God who gives us the free will to choose, and now we have taken it to such unimaginable levels.

I found ways to rationalize most everything I did and excused it as a male, cultural or ethnic thing—not so anymore. For about a year or so I would pray and ask God to help me to be more like him, to imitate him and to know him. Then I would sit and read the Bible for 1/2 to 1 hour almost every night. It wasn't until a few months ago that I made the connection, and now see that reading the Bible is how I was getting to know him. He was working on me and I didn't even know it. Changing me, and transforming me to the point where I am not as judgmental as I used to be.

Jennifer Lopez had a revealing dress on for an awards show which I did not see live, but subsequently saw a picture in a newspaper article. While I could admire the shape of her feminine form, I could now do so without any lustful thoughts! Was I really being transformed this much? Even though she has issues to resolve, who am I to judge others with sins far greater than hers?

During the retreat I was asked what I needed a prayer for, and I honestly didn't know, but said I would leave it in God's hands. I received way more than I could ever dream possible. The morning after I actually saw that elusive light shining in through my window. Brighter than anything I had ever seen. All this time I thought it was just a myth. All my confusion on matters vanished.

Everything in life that mattered had become crystal clear as I came into this new reality of the existence of God. All my priorities were instantly rearranged. Something I had read earlier made more sense now. The Holy Spirit enlightens us mainly with the information we already have within us. I had spent many nights reading and now as all the junk was being purged from my mind, a new deeper understanding of all was now making sense.

All I could think was "WOW—Jesus, it is you and your alive and this is what you did for me and everyone; by dying on the cross." It all hit me so fast and hard (now I understand the meaning of the bigger they are the harder they fall, I had fallen hard.) This was immediately followed by overwhelming feelings of unworthiness as I saw my sins in front of me for what they really were.

All this because of my faithful ancestors and now I must be faithful to my descendants. There is no shame to suffer for being called a Christian. Praise God for the privilege of being a member of his family and being called by his wondrous name. (1 Peter 4)

During this transformation process I am now becoming a Spiritual Robin Hood of sorts; taking from God's message of life and light and giving to those in spiritual darkness.

To the glory of our Lord, Jesus Christ. Alleluia!

To my dearest Martha,
Even after discovering the Father's unconditional love for
me, it took me a while to realize that I never experienced
that type of love for another human being, or knew it
was possible, until you came into my life.

God is good!

To my cousin Lourdes,
She stepped out and challenged me to find out more
about my own faith before venturing out to search
others. I have discovered everything I need right here,
in my own Catholic home and in the process I know
in my heart:

I've found a meaning to life.

To Evangeline, (Vangie)
God's little 'fire cracker' reaching out and spreading
herself over vast areas. Yet, she made time to explode in
my life long enough to help in my walk with the Lord.
Not only was she an endless supply of information, she
helped keep me scripturally sound as well as filling in
missing commas during this journey that showed me:

*The Father's love is the only true path
to our Glorious Transformation.*

Introduction

I have been asked on more than one occasion by Catholic friends the purpose of writing these notes and why I feel compelled to share them with others. I was very fortunate in the beginning to have been counseled by a very wise, spirit filled priest, who after hearing my confession and seeing what I was going through said, "You must give witness to others." I thought to myself, "what does he mean, get up in front of people and groups and tell them my story?" Needless to say, I was mortified. I don't give speeches or speak well in front of any group of people without going through cold sweats and becoming physically ill. I prayed about it and asked, "Why Lord?" He promptly answered as he led me to open the Bible to Corinthians and there it was in black and white. "Once you have been graced by the power of the Holy Spirit, you will give witness or you will start to lose these graces." That did not appeal to me, but on the flip side, it said "Once you start to give witness, you will receive more of my graces and an increase of my anointing." Call me greedy, but I want more. But addition to this, in John (19:35) we are called to testify so that others may believe.

If you recall Resurrection Sunday, (Easter Sunday to Catholics) Jesus rose from the dead and now is very much alive and actively working through those people who are willing to become empty vessels for his Holy Spirit to work through them and empowering and giving them a new boldness to spread the Good News.

Jesus wants to reveal himself to anyone who will accept him and he will make his reality known in new and different ways to everyone. Ways humans can not even fathom.

I still consider myself a baby Christian in this respect, even though I am a life-long Catholic of 45 years—half of those years a Catholic in name only. That does not matter to Christ, because he himself spent his time on earth ministering to the sick, the tax collectors, cheats, prostitutes and the like.

Seek and you shall find. Those Words have taken on a whole new meaning in my life. Wouldn't you know, the ratio of those actively seeking Jesus to those that will, in fact, find him are 1:1. Try to beat those odds in anything else in this life. Unfortunately, the ratio of those not actively seeking Christ to those that are is least 1,000:1. I guess we have our work cut out for us.

At the end of this booklet is God's Plan for Salvation for us along with a "Commitment Prayer" or as some call it, "The Sinners Prayer." That's right, 'Personal Salvation,' it's not just for those other Christians, but for Catholic's as well. We are all followers of Christ. Committing our life to Christ and having him come and live in us. In effect, re-establishing that direct line of communication that humans were inherently created with, but unfortunately lost by our first parents, Adam & Eve through original sin that made us spiritually dead. Come alive again. It's our choice and no one can do it for us. When we die from this world, our souls will live for an eternity in a new heavenly body. The only choice for us is where to spend that eternity and there are only two choices. (Hint: one of those is with our God.)

Please don't get me wrong, I am not holier than thou, and if anything, this special anointing has magnified all my sins from the past and the present, and I only ask to bear with me as I do my best to follow God's ways. But first, I have to know what those ways are, so hence my journey continues into his Word.

Friends,

I have before you a document I was led to write.

Part 1 is outlined a message to the young people of our Church. A message of my witness on receiving God's abundant outpouring of his presence and love of which he is waiting to pour out on all who ask.

Next is a very simple message for our youth to get them more involved and excited about praying and praising Jesus.

I am personally bringing this message to as many youth group leaders as I can in order to get the message out. Please look it over and use the parts you can as it is an outline and should be tailored to your own needs.

Part 2 is my entire understanding of my Catholic/ Christian faith as I know it today. I hope it motivates you on your own personal journey.

Part 3 is a further enlightenment of Catholic Doctrine and relationships with God as well as with one another and my understanding of how they have affected me.

God Bless you all for your attention on this message.

Part 1

Witness

I attended a Retreat in December '99 led by a very vibrant spirit filled leader, Sr. Nancy Kellar. Her very first session talked about the joy and love of God for his people, which up to that time were only distant words I could not relate to. During the prayer and worship that followed, everyone could feel the love and presence of the Lord in the room. It even got to me—and the two women sitting next to me laid their hands on me and said they could feel the spirit wanting to grace me with his presence. It was so close I could almost touch it. And as a man, (which in this instance makes us the weaker gender) I pulled back and resisted at the last moment and immediately after the session went back to my room and cried tears of joy as the most joyful experiences of my life were flashing before my eyes. As if to say this is only a hint of the love I feel for you.

The afternoon session that followed ended with everyone being prayed over and I was asked what I needed prayer for in my life. Being at a loss as to how to proceed, I told the prayer group I wasn't sure what I needed but that God knows me better than I know myself so I would leave it in his hands to give me what I needed. As they started to pray I went into a trance-like state and one of them said they could feel the power of the Holy Spirit flowing through her to me! Again at the last instance of complete surrender, I felt myself break away and resist. The last session of the day was a powerful session ending with prayer, worship and song—but again I fell short of achieving my goal.

Saturday night I prayed to God to let me know him and feel him and asked for his guidance. I became silent for several minutes and then reached over and picked up the Bible lying on the bed. I opened it to Daniel in the Old Testament. With the exception of Genesis, I had never read anything in the Old Testament, but there on the top of the page was a story with my estranged-wife's name at the top and with trembling hands I picked up the Bible and started reading. It seemed my deepest, darkest secret was being revealed to me. The one obstacle, sin or shame that in MY mind was making me unworthy and was blocking any attempts for the spirit to enter me were revealed. I stayed up most of the night thinking "How could this be, why hadn't I seen it before?"

Needless to say, the next morning I sought Father Al and told him of my need for reconciliation, repentance and I saw my worst fears and worries subside as I made myself right with the Lord and was now ready to receive him.

What I relearned was that the first step to receiving the Lord was repentance. God wants us and is waiting to pour his abundant, overflowing grace on us. His love *is there*, it always has been and will be forever. My sins have already been forgiven nailed on Christ's Cross—I just never got it. For anyone feeling unwanted, unloved or that they were mistakes in this life, know this: he loved us, embraced us and had a plan for us, even before we were ever conceived so it doesn't matter what circumstances brought us into the world. Our lives are our gift from God.

The only thing holding us back from feeling that pure, unconditional love is ourselves. The only thing blocking us is our lack of repentance, desire or preconceived feelings of inadequacy. He loves us so much and wants us to share in that communion with him.

The morning after the retreat, back home, everything in life I now see with a new perspective, new zeal and with new meaning. My purpose is so much clearer as are my priorities. Even the comics seem funnier and little expressions have more meaning. Such as "Watch out what you wish for."Forgive me for thinking or even saying this, but the morning after the retreat I wanted to ask the Holy Spirit to just *back off,* because I felt I was going to explode with his presence and love.

Again, the only obstacle I saw to my personal relationship was myself. All I had to do was open my heart, examine my soul and conscious and it came. **My Baptism in the Spirit, my salvation, the day I saw the light and was born again, or my personal day of Pentecost.**

After you are Baptized with water, God the Father, God the Son and God the Holy Spirit, The Trinity begins to live within us and we take them everywhere thereafter.

During Confirmation, although for most this will be a transparent process, God's Love is being poured into our hearts through the Holy Spirit, which has been given to us.

As we yield our lives to the management of the Holy Spirit, he brings supernatural enlightenment of Jesus into our Spirit. He helps us to understand ourselves and shows us how to live.

We will know and believe the love God has for us. God is Love and he who abides in love abides in God and God abides in us.

What is next? The Baptism of the Holy Spirit? Is this a new Sacrament? No. It is the further release of the power of the Holy Spirit already within us that you will receive by faith at your Confirmation or sometime thereafter. It has only taken me 45 years to get to this point, How long will it take for each of you? Now in my experience, it has enabled me to live the Christian life I wanted to live but had only partial success in doing. You will begin to experience a new ability to appreciate Jesus, the Bible, our daily prayer life and our faith through this living experience.

Confirmation

I have seen the light, I'm saved, I'm home free. It's done and I can sit back and relax. Almost immediately after those thoughts crossed my mind I realized, this is only the beginning of a new life. I'm not holier than any one here. The only thing the holy spirit has done is shown me the light and I still have to walk the straight and narrow more then ever if I'm going to make it. He's shown me the way, but I remain with this free will to choose between Good and Evil.

Don't go around hurting each other and calling each other names, gossiping, backstabbing. You drive a nail in their heart/soul every time you do. Sure you can apologize to your parents, teachers, spouses, siblings and remove that nail, but what are you left with after that? Don't give in to the choice of leaving that hole behind. Why not instead, use some of that tried and true parental reverse psychology? When someone approaches you with a thought, idea or project they are thinking about try positively enforcing them by saying, "Great idea, I know you will make it work and I look forward to seeing it!" We would probably blow them away and start them thinking positively about themselves thinking, "Wow, I better follow through on this and give it my best or I will look foolish."

Sex, it's a grand thing. Everybody is doing it. It's on T.V. and radio, in romance novels and teen magazines, which explain the many ways to please your lover and satisfy yourself. Girls, your imagination grows wild as you start to dream of the perfect encounter and plan, prepare the right time, the right outfit and place for the ultimate climax. Then as the hour approaches (just as Y2K with its anticipated promises, uncertainties, parties and hoopla) you hold your breath as the clock strikes midnight. Your Y2K turns into an anticlimactic event. It's over and leaves you wondering what happened ?

Guys are hormone driven at this age and what frequently happens is he's gotten what he wants and dumps you. Or every date there after has to end with the "act" or he won't love you anymore!

Look deep into the eyes of your friends talking about their sexual encounters. You'll see a vast emptiness of lost hopes and promises. At that point in time you realize it's not all it's hyped up to be.

But when you join together in marriage and establish a covenant, or take a vow, in front of God and all your friends and relatives to join with this spouse that is making a life-long commitment to your mutual happiness and is expressing an unconditional love that will look beyond any physical weaknesses we all have. The sex act becomes a very meaningful event and every time you come together you are renewing that covenant you established when you took the vows. Our great God in all his infinite mercy and grace did create it to be a pleasurable experience for us at this time.

None of you kids chose the parents you have. None of your parents specifically chose you (unless you were adopted). During that renewal of the covenant God may bless you with a Gift of Life. He gave that to us, chose us and paired us up with the parents we have in his infinite wisdom and knowledge; he has a plan and purpose for where he specifically placed us.

Watch movie Simon Birch

Many people don't see that life as a gift from God. Under the wrong circumstances it become an inconvenience, a thorn in your side and will disrupt the plans and lifestyle you made for yourself. After all it's your body. Well guess what? God gave us the free will to choose. That's right, he gave us the free will to choose. To choose him, his ways and his teachings or those of his fallen angels. How can these heavenly beings possibly have turned away from God? Because in his infinite wisdom and mercy he also gave them the same free will to choose him. He doesn't want to force his will upon anybody. You have to choose him. Well why are they down here reeking havoc and tempting us, this master deceiver. Well, everyone knows misery loves company and Satan knows he has already been defeated. It's been prophesized, it's in the Bible and he wants all the company he can get.

"But don't listen to me, I'm not young enough to know everything!"

Mass and the Eucharist

But we are just teens, who are we going to convince and/or evangelize? The number one thing we do together at Church is come together every week on Sundays. The number one complaint from your peers that I hear is "It's so boring, so ritualistic, I don't understand what is going on—and a lot of adults fall in this category or also need to be reminded—or it's music I can't relate to." Traditional religion to them seems to be dead. We need a new, powerful, dynamic, living, contemporary christianity.

Why not host a Mass. "The perfect mass" for your fellow catechist and peers? Where you can narrate what is going on and pick some contemporary music to excite them.

Example:

1. Narrator: (prior to the start of mass) Introductory rites consists of songs and prayers which come before the Liturgy of the Word of God and Christ's presence when the bread and wine are transformed into the Body and Blood of Christ.

2a) Narrator: (prior to the first reading) First we listen to the first reading from the Hebrew Bible, the Old Testament (BC.) Since the Church sees all prophesy, promises and aspirations of ancient Hebrew fulfilled in Christ, we must read the Old Testament in order to understand its Christian interpretation in the New Testament.

2b) Narrator: (immediately after the first reading) In the New Testament we will hear as the Priest reads the Gospel, that which deals directly with God's manifestation (power) in Jesus Christ who is present and speaking to us through the Word.

3a) Narrator: (just before the consecration) All kneel in adoration as our Lord and our God comes before this altar. Oh Jesus, bread from Heaven. How immense is your goodness. Raise our faith in your real presence of the Eucharist. You who selflessly totally transform yourself into this unheard of miracle. This consecrated matter of bread and wine into your body and blood. Increase our faith in you in this blessed sacrament daily. Excite in us a hunger and thirst of the Eucharistic food that according to your Word, "taking this heavenly bread we can enjoy true life now and forever.

4a) Narrator:(prior to receiving Holy Communion) When we receive Holy Communion, we are not really worthy to receive it. None of us are, but the Eucharist is given precisely to make us holy, to make us worthy. We should want it as often as possible.

4b) Lord only say the Word and I shall be healed. You promised as we consume your body and blood you would heal us as we surrender our anger, frustrations, unforgiveness or any things we have failed to do.

5. Narrator: (After the blessing) Go in peace. That new inner peace we feel now that we've been rejuvenated in body, mind and spirit are now in perfect harmony and we are free, more open to praise and worship God the rest of the week through our thoughts, Words and deeds.

6. (Optional) Prayer teams can assemble in back of church. Kids come and ask for help for yourself or struggling friends. Families come and pray together for a stronger family bond or pray for a distant family member. Start and/or renew a new tradition of family prayer today!

The Bible

How do we find out what his Word is for us? By reading
the Bible and not just any Bible. (Does everyone know
and understand Shakespeare?) One and a half years ago,
I was given a King James version but in reading that
version, I had to try and figure out what was being said
before I could figure out what was being said. Get an
N.I.V. or my favorite "Catholic Living Bible", it talks to
you in plain English. Just find one that speaks to you.
Don't be afraid of it, after all the Catholic Church first
put it together around 399 A.D.

A recent Bible passage I read John 6:53 said "He that eats
my flesh and drinks my blood, dwells in me and I in Him
and shall have eternal life. Soon after I read that I received
a new deeper understanding. Sure, to Catholics the
Eucharist is the obvious answer that comes to mind, the
physical manifestation of the body and blood of Christ.

More than ever I am now convinced of his presence in
the Eucharist and whenever I receive him as such, I ask
him to displace that part of my heart with a like amount
of his body and blood I take in during communion. (Jn
3:10) He must become greater and greater and I must
become less and less. As St. Therese of Lisieux once said
" He does not come down from Heaven every day just
to lie in a golden Ciborium. He comes to find another
heaven which is infinitely dearer to Him, the heaven of
our souls, created in his image, the living temples of his
spirit melded with ours by virtue of accepting him as
our Lord and Savior."

But at the same time, or in addition to that we know Jesus is Emmanuel, God with us. And we know he was the Word made flesh, then it suddenly hit me, *"He is the Word!"* So, in order to really know him, get into his mind, know his will, imitate him, we need to get into his Word. We need to devour it, consume it and drink it in, allowing it to saturate us completely. What an awesome enlightenment. The incarnation was God becoming human so that we humans could become more like him.

May our lives serve merely as a witness to his love. Who would have ever thought reading the Bible would turn out to be so much fun, especially when we have the Holy Spirit guiding us and explaining it as we go along.

Everything we need to live the Christian Life is contained in the Bible. How to treat others, relationships, respect for life, how to handle money and so on. But, who better to give us a blueprint for living than he who gave us our lives? If we think back on events in our lives that did not go well, we probably did not try to handle them in a scriptural fashion. But when we live the life he has intended for us and according to his will, life really does get uncomplicated.

Read what Revelations says about the second coming and how it is going to transpire. Because there will be many signs and many false prophets telling you "this is it," but you will be prepared, you will know. It will be unmistakable. The skies will part and his face will show through and he will ask all of us again. Will you accept me? Will you follow me? It is hard to imagine at that point people will still not believe and Christ will once again say: *"Is that your final answer?"* And people will go about their business, seeking their own selfish pleasures.

He will then place a seal on top of the opening where his light is shining through and everyone will really know that was it, no more chances. Everyone will realize the error of their ways, but by then, it will be too late for them. (Matthew 13:41) I will send my angels and they will separate, out of the kingdom, every temptation and all who are evil, and throw them into the furnace and burn them. There shall be weeping and gnashing of teeth.

—They will be there for all eternity.

On a Saturday, 1-15-2000, I had a wake-up call about 3:00 a.m. from the Holy Spirit and he was telling me, "So what are you going to do with all this information you have been gathering?" I really didn't know and as I got up out of bed, made some coffee, I got out a pad of paper, and pen as he started dictating the above message to me. Twelve hand written pages and two hours later, I started typing and couldn't believe what was unfolding before me! I have tried shooting holes in the message and have questioned almost every bit of and prayed about it, and darn if he doesn't reveal the answer to me in one form or another! Since that Saturday morning, as I receive a deeper understanding or a new experience or enlightenment, I will continue to document them into this ever growing message.

The biggest concern I had was with the "sex talk" portion and asked if it was really appropriate to have that in here. Again, I prayed about it and the very next day during a radio broadcast two Christian women are talking about the same thing. They went on to say our kids are already receiving the message from other sources such as: school, kids, television, radio, as well as other Ungodly sources. Why shouldn't they then be told the Christian views, or in our case, the Catholic views about sexuality.

How can you argue with that?

Part 2

On the last day of a 10-week seminar entitled, "Life in the Spirit", we had as a featured speaker Sr. Patricia O'Brien from Edelweiss House. She started talking about the need for prayer and finding time in our busy lives for prayer. Her Words were not making any sense to me for some reason. I just could not comprehend or could even relate to what she was saying. Then, it dawned on me, "find time to pray, Lord I have not found time to stop praying. You are in my thoughts, words and deeds from the time I wake in the morning to the time I go to sleep."

Then she asked if we had to would we give our lives to the cause just as some people have done in recent church and school shootings. I am ashamed to say I might not have and would have cowered in some corner to avoid giving my life for Christ as he had for us. But now, after realizing that our lives are a gift from God, how could I ever deny him what is already his, "take me home Jesus."

Her next topic was on the need to evangelize, but we had to be careful because we would be confronted by all types of people and needed to be prepared by reading the Bible first and catechism books and be ready for any objections. I thought that sounded reasonable as I had already made it a priority to read the Bible since it has become so alive to me. But now I kept hearing a voice inside of me that said, "Bring my children back to me." I would say, "Lord you heard the sister, I have to study, take quizzes and past the test first." But again I heard "Bring my sheep back to me." Now, it has taken me 45 years to get to this point and I am slow but I am starting to realize sometimes you just have to sit and listen to what is being said. Then it hit me, Lord you are talking about me and people like me that are going through difficult times in their lives through a loss of a loved one, or illness or any of life's frustrations. The first thing we do is walk away from you and become bitter, angry, resentful and sometimes dangerous. We need to be on the watch for this and sometimes just lend an ear and listen to them.

I went through a similar circumstance and started seeing doctors who gave me sleeping pills, anxiety pills and Prozac, then would say, hope you feel better, see you next month. They were giving me everything I wanted, everything I asked for, but nothing I needed. Then came along a coworker who asked how I was doing. I laid into her so hard with my problems I'm surprised I didn't scare her off. A few weeks later I ran into her again and gave her my tales of woes and pity, "poor me, poor me." She listened and as she was leaving said, "I'll pray for you." About this time I was open to anything that would have come my way as I was searching for answers. If a Jehovah witness showed up at my doorstep, I probably would have let him in and asked him "what took so long, let me start some coffee and we'll talk." Or worse, I could have received a call from a Mormon who would entice me with their doctrine, "sorry you're losing a wife, but hey, if you join us you could have two." Worse yet, the most dangerous new "cult" would have come along, and probably made sense to me, as they are making sense to a lot of lost souls out there (for example, the New Age Group). Except now I realize I was born May 16, a Taurus, and us Taurus' don't believe in that new age bunk.

Of course this is a play on words since in (Deut 18:10-11) it states, "all forms of Divination and anyone doing these things is an object of horror and disgust to the Lord." This includes witchcraft, black magic, fortune telling, mediums, wizards, calling forth spirits of the dead, horoscopes, astrology, clairvoyants, palm, tea leaf or tarot card readers, psychics, santeros, spirit guides, witchdoctors, voodoo and assorted occult games. Many of these things are featured in Harry Potter movies and should be avoided.

A few weeks later that same coworker came back, much to my surprise, and said "I think I know of a place where you will find what you need. Would you meet me and my fiancée for a 9 a.m. service at our Christian Church?" And I thought, can I do that, is it legal? After all I am a Catholic, but I went and started listening to their message and uplifting music. Most of the time I just stood or sat in the back, in the shadows and silently wept as the message of the Lord started touching me.

You see, you don't need a lot of bible study to bring back his sheep, because for the most part the foundation has already been laid so you will not get caught up in doctrinal or scriptural debates you may not be able to answer. The seed has already been planted and it just needs us to add a little water and nurturing to help it grow again. Bring back his stray sheep. I can do that *now*. So sister was half-right because I still do need to study his Word, but that lack of knowledge won't slow me down from re-evangelizing his people.

Finally, she gave us a talk on the need to tithe and give the Lord his share of our earnings. I'm sorry to say there was a time when I would have said "Lord here they come again, those beggars are after my hard earned money. If you want ten percent then help me win that lottery jackpot and maybe I'll slip you a ten." Now if I were to acquire a lottery ticket and come up with a gazillion dollars, I may *keep* ten percent and give him the rest, *why?* Well, because I need the write-off and if anyone has been paying attention to any of the above, I'm not talking about the write-off to IRS or the federal government, but to God to make up for my past, current or future unworthiness and sinful ways. And I now know it is humanly impossible to out give him. He may turn around and send me two gazillion dollars or bless me in ways the human mind can't even fathom.

To summarize what I just said I would like to illustrate by using the following example: A woman is looking for a coat to go with a new outfit even though she has several coats at home already. Instead she goes to the children's section and purchases 3 or 4 coats with the same money because she remembers a story about needy kids in an orphanage. These coats now become part of her prayer, or an answer to a prayer the kids have. But she doesn't stop there. Instead of putting them in a drop box, she personally delivers them to an orphanage in an area of the city which is less than desirable, at some personal risk to herself (risking her life doing Christs' work). But she doesn't stop there either she has also brought along a children's bible and reads them a few stories (starting their evangelization process). Finally, the coats which were part of her prayers have also become part of her tithe to God! Thus closing the loop in a perfect circle of life in Christ. This is just one example and the combinations are limited only by our imaginations. *Praise the Lord!*

Midway through this ten-week session, almost everyone in our small group discussion including myself has expressed concern and fear over what God would ask of us or what we may have to give up. Our fears of what God may ask are greater than what he actually will ask. We must be willing to surrender all, including this fear, to learn that God usually takes only the things that are obstacles to our living this life to the fullest. He purifies much of what he takes, returns it to us, and then we have more than before.

> *Give God the bad and he will make it good!*
> *Give God the Good and he will make it better!*
> *Give God the better and he will make it best!*

1-28-2000
In this past week I have come into a deeper understanding of my faith.

The only thing keeping me from a further anointing of the Holy Spirit is my own lack of knowledge, primarily, his Word. The anointing is released through the knowledge of God's Word. It only operates with what we know and no more. We can all increase this anointing by increasing our knowledge of God's Word. In effect, arming ourselves with the full armor of God's Word to increase our anointing in our battle with the master deceiver. Our knowledge of the full gospel in all areas needs to increase day by day.

My dear friends from work who helped guide me through my new spiritual life, one a Christian Methodist, the other a Nazarene. The Nazarene kept dwelling on all the coming prophesized disasters up to and including the end time. And I saw his point and learned so that I may understand and recognize the real coming of Christ and have moved on. Looking now at my friend, he is still stuck two years later watching, waiting, and preparing for the end times. He has even gone so far as to build a cabin with generators, kerosene lamps and well water. He is completely secluded in the hills of Kentucky. He can't seem to leave that mindset and move on.

My Christian coworker has come upon some personal problems of his own and has, it seems, temporarily turned away from God. But again, two years later, he is still quoting the same 3–5 bible verses he always has. The more people I talk to, I find they believe in Jesus, but not that "healing stuff" or "resting in the Spirit" or don't want to think about the end times. How can we, who have so much, believe in so little! When others involved in the occult, magic, witchcraft or new age have so little and can believe in so much! Many followers of Christ believe in the principle that God still heals, and it's a good theory, but they have so much trouble with its practice. Given, healings and miracles are a dramatic answer to prayer, but we have such an awesome God for whom nothing is impossible.

When did our Bible, his Word, become an a-la-carte book where you can pick and choose the sections to believe in? The whole book is his Word! Take all or nothing!

Then I came to the understanding that going to the Christian Church, like I have been, with their praise and worship styles I love so dearly are making me into a more complete Catholic. They have many ministries for practical everyday living. But in and of itself it is not complete. I need the Sacraments afforded through the Catholic Church and believe in them with all my heart and soul. But that is no longer enough. Their blinders are also on and for most people what they are getting is enough. And that's O.K.

But I am starting to realize the various Christian denominations are like my friends who pick and choose which area of the Bible they want to specialize in while tending to overlook parts of the whole gospel. Until my understanding becomes deeper, I will continue to worship and pray at both denominations along with the limited charismatic functions available in this area and pray they might someday meld to where they will not only preach, but practice the whole gospel. "Jesus as the savior, the healer, the baptizer and the coming King along with all the sacraments." His Word and his promises are the same—*Yesterday, Today and Forever.*

3-1-00

From a conference retreat one exercise we experienced, a Word of knowledge was given to me by my partner was *"apple."* Along with that she saw a vision of a boy 6 to 8 years old.

I seem to forget the Holy Spirit is a person, a being. He is one of the Godhead, the Trinity. God the Father—God the Son—God the Holy Spirit. To know him is to love him. He is not just the Spirit of Jesus within us, but the one Jesus sent to be our comforter, our teacher, our guide.

An illustration by Sr. Nancy Kellar given to me a month ago I am only now being led to understand as follows. "Across a long foggy canyon there is a tightrope leading to the other side. My dear friend asks if I think he can cross it on a bike. Half-heartedly I say, "Sure, Go for it." He does it and then comes back! He again asks if I think he can do it again and this time I say most assuredly Yes! I've already seen you do it. So he replies, "OK. Get on the back!" At the end of the dark canyon, through the fog and into the unknown is God, who our faith tells us "he is there awaiting you." Jesus is the cyclist sent to bring us to Him. The tightrope is the Holy Spirit, with the direct line of communication to God!

Man was originally created with the ability to have this intimate, direct line of open communication with God, but Adam and Eve lost that ability for us through the Original Sin. Hence the song, *Amazing Grace,* "I once was lost and now I'm found, was blind, but now I see." The spirit within us is lost or hidden. When we are saved, that direct line of communication is re-established, our direct link to God by the person of the Holy Spirit.

As everything is coming together for me, understanding the magnitude of what was lost by this one act caused me to resent our original parents. The only commandment they had to consciously obey was not to eat from the Tree of Knowledge of good and evil. Today, we have to face decisions in our everyday lives of choosing with the knowledge of good and evil. Evil today is disguised in all forms and cleverly packaged by the evil one who is still very much with us today.

And all because of that darn apple in the Garden of Eden, which was part of the root cause of my memory of Adam and Eve and the Apple. Around the age of 6 or 8, my teacher told me about what happened and I never made the connection of what the magnitude of what was actually lost through that act. But now I have this sense that I need to forgive Adam and Eve. Talk about your intergenerational forgiveness.

Adam and Eve, I forgive you!

Recently I fell asleep reading a small book written by George E. Schulhoff, a man who has been able to hear God's voice ever since he was very young. It is second nature to him and he could not imagine living any other way. As I awoke from my nap with no one else in the house, no windows open or appliances or audio/video equipment turned on I was startled by a very soft clear voice in my ear that simply said, "I love you" I couldn't believe it, I sat up immediately and said, "No fair!" I was just getting up and wanted to hear more and you caught me off guard. Could it really have been you God? Our God does not mince words. He only says what needs to be said in His own time. His timing is perfect. Even when he was on this earth, he did not partake in idle chatter or gossip. I now know I have to be alert for when the time comes again, and be ready to listen and obey.

On the way back from Chicago one night, I was approximately an hour and a half from home driving on I-65 about 2a.m. because I needed to get home that night. Driving in my 13 year old van cruising at 65 mph on a lonely country stretch and it was pitch black. All of a sudden, both headlights went out at the same time (don't you just hate when that happens). I started to panic a little, wondering what my next move would be. One option I did not want to take was to pull over in the middle of nowhere. Just ahead was a semi-trailer so I sped up some to get behind him and take advantage of his lights until I could figure out what to do. After about ten minutes of weighing my options, it finally dawned on me to pray for a solution. Much to my amazement after a few minutes both lights came back on. I was still skeptical as to whether they would remain on until I could reach the next exit or should I just continue home.

I opted to continue and, much to my amazement, made it safely home!

At work that day, I told a mechanic friend about the problem with the lights and hoped he could offer a solution. He said it was just probably corrosion on the negative leads from the battery. What a cheap fix. I went home and wire brushed the connections after making sure the lights still did not work, which they didn't. So 15 minutes later after everything was put back together, I pulled the light switch and everything worked fine. The next day I gave the whole story to my friend and his matter of fact reaction was, "Our God got you home safely and then led you to me for the repair!"

The love God has for his children is so outrageous, it's beyond any human comprehension. He gives us the things we need if we only ask him and pray with an expectant prayer. No, he will not always give us what we want, what father gives his child everything he asks for? Not if you don't want to have a spoiled child. But we do everything within our means to supply the basic needs for our children. Our basic needs will always be met and sometimes even lavishly by our heavenly father. In time, I hope to be praying with that expectancy that my needs will be met and not seem so surprised when they are. *What an awesome God!*

There's Something About Mary

But what could it be. The movie of the same title starring Cameron Diaz did not provide the answers I was seeking. The preeminent role of Mary in God's plan for salvation needs to be understood. "In Mary is found all the life and happiness God can give a mere creature and all that a mere creature is capable of receiving." Mary is God's Supreme Masterpiece and being our Mother, she wants to share with us that fullness of God's life and happiness we are capable of receiving.

Can you imagine being picked to have your body, your womb be a living tabernacle to our God for nine months? Official Catholic teaching has never considered beliefs about Mary as being equal in importance to truths about God the Father, Son and Holy Spirit. And in the Gospel of Mark, Mary was cast in a negative light along with Jesus' other relatives who did not understand him or his mission. This is not surprising though, because no one really understood Jesus or his mission, until his crucifixion.

It is a tragic fact that beliefs about Mary, the Mother of Jesus, have become a source of division among Christians and many Catholics who don't understand our own Church teachings about Mary. Sadly I was one of them until recently.

At a recent retreat of about 150–180 people, during our last anointing with oil, I noticed a very pleasant odor that reminded me of a bouquet of roses! About 4–5 others in the group also noticed the same fragrance and we all went up to the person administering the oil to find out what kind of oil he was using. His eyes welled up with tears as he told us it was just plain oil, nothing in it and he invited us to smell for ourselves, which we did. I told others of this marvelous experience which as of yet, I did not understand. And they went up to be annointed but did not receive the same sensation. It was then one of the women said it was a sign, meant for me and the handful of others in the room. A message from Mary!

I later found out this Holy Oil was blessed during an apparition of Our Lady at Medjugorje in Bosnia where our Lady has been appearing since 1981. The oil was placed on the altar in the home of the Visionary (Mary can only be seen by one or a small handful of people). During this appearance, Our Lady came on a cloud, which covered the altar, including the oil that was placed there. Our Lady gave her blessing to all who asked her and she blessed the oil during that visit. I immediately acquired a small container of the same oil for myself. I don't know if I'll ever receive that beautiful fragrance again, but in my case that once was enough. She made a believer out of me and I now have an adoration and devotion to her I never thought I would have.

Her basic message throughout the years at Lourdes, Fatima, Guadalupe and now Medjugorje (by the way there is only one Mary and she appears to the local people in a form and dress they can relate to) is basically always the same. "Pray for peace, conversions, penance, fasting and read the Bible," "Pray for an end to abortion" and keep "Praising and worshiping my son Jesus" Her message verbatim of Feb 25, 2000 is as follows:

"Dear Children! Wake up from the sleep of unbelief and sin; because this is a time of grace which God gives you. Use this time and seek the grace of healing of your heart from God, so that you may see God and man with the heart. Pray in a special way for those who have not come to know God's love, and witness with your life so that they also can come to know God and His immeasurable love. Thank you for having responded to my call."

3-25-00

"Pray and make good use of this time, because this is a time of grace. I am with you and I intercede for each one of you before God, for your heart to open to God and to God's love. Little children, pray without ceasing, until prayer becomes a joy for you. Thank you for having responded to my call."

Mary's role in God's plan was prophetically expressed in the Old Testament. In the book of Genesis 3:15 and Isaiah 7:14 along with several mentions throughout the new testament where Matthew 1:22 presents Jesus' birth to Mary as a fulfillment of this prophecy. Mary is also referenced in Revelations 12. Mary was full of faith and in Luke 1:38 declares " I am the servant of the Lord. Let it be done to me as you say." Mary is the new Eve, reversing the first Eve's "no" to God. By the disobedience of Eve, all mankind became immersed in the bondage of sin. Mary's obedience to God opened the way for the saving work of Jesus. Mary always devoted her life to doing the will of God. She followed her son from the beginning to the end of his life.

At Cana, (John 2:1-12), where her simple firm faith evoked Jesus' first miracle. This scene gives us a glimpse of Mary's role of intercession—that she is able to approach Jesus with the needs of others and she is heard for her faith. After Jesus had declined to help at the wedding at Cana because his time had not yet come, his mother sent the servants back to him with instructions to do exactly as he says. I can just picture Jesus looking up at his mother and thinking "Aw Mom" as he honored his earthly mother by following through and changing the water into the finest wine available.

New testament records that Mary received the Holy Spirit when she conceived Jesus, thus making her the first recipient of the Holy Spirit, and consequently, the first Christian! Mary may be the mother of Jesus, but why ours? It is based on the passage when Jesus saw his mother and the disciple whom he loved standing near while he hung on the cross, he said to his mother, "Woman, behold your son!" Then he said to the disciple, "Behold, your Mother." Catholics do not pray to Mary or worship her. Worship belongs only to God. We do ask Mary to pray for us, and believe that her intercession has a great effect in calling forth God's grace and mercy. But this is because of her special relationship with Jesus, not because of her own merits. Nothing Mary does merits or gives salvation. Like us, Mary only cooperates with God's grace and his saving plan. Her special role as an intercessor, a model disciple, and a mother to believers, only stems from God's sovereign choice and from his grace.

This special grace that enabled Mary to become the Mother of God is called Mary's *Immaculate Conception*. It is the belief that arose among the early Christians that God had preserved Mary from the inheritance of original sin passed on to all mankind from our first parents from the moment she was conceived. Mary did not have an extraordinary birth, as Jesus did, she had a normal human mother and father and was conceived and born in a normal way. This was God's perfect act of purification to prepare Mary to bear the Son of God in her womb. This special grace is more of a statement about Jesus than about Mary. It proclaims that Jesus was someone so unique and holy that God would even prepare his mother for his birth by preserving her from sin. The book of Genesis implies that Mary was preserved from sin by the free gift of God so she would not be bound to experience the consequences of sin and death in the same way we do. Her assumption into Heaven might be understood as a sign of what might have happened at the end of all our lives had Adam and Eve not sinned.

The most common prayer among Catholics is the *Hail Mary* consisting of three parts...

"Hail Mary full of grace, the Lord is with thee, blessed are thou amongst women,"

—words spoken by the Archangel Gabriel
(Lk1:28)

"Blessed is the fruit of thy womb with Jesus,"

—words spoken by her cousin Elizabeth under the inspiration of the Holy Spirit through John the Baptist who was in her womb.

(could it be that John received the Baptism of the Holy Spirit while still in his mother's womb?)

"Holy Mary, Mother of God, pray for us sinners now and at the hour of our death, Amen."
—a formula of petition

Mary is so misunderstood and if people only knew her. If anything she was and remains Jesus' biggest fan and his loudest cheerleader!

The Promise

At a recent prayer meeting, the woman sitting next to me and I received a sweet scent of Lilies that seemed to permeate the entire room. But as we looked around the entire room, we noticed no flowers or air fresheners, then we looked at each other and smiled. It became more special when we later found out we were the only ones to receive that scent and she explained a Bible verse I later found in Songs (2:1), "I am the rose of Sharon, the lily of the valley." Jesus was actually among us! Although I didn't need that smell to know he was among us, it sure was reassuring. What an awesome experience and hint of things to come when we reach Heaven.

Life in Heaven will be so spectacular and so satisfying to the deepest longing of our souls, we can hardly grasp it. When the Bible tells us about God making the heavens and the earth in the beginning, He was speaking only of the physical realm of the earth and outer space. The spiritual dimension already existed (The second Heaven). God had already been the "I Am." After this is a third Heaven or paradise that exists. That is where God resides and where Christ sits at his right hand.

Prior to Jesus' death and resurrection, righteous people who died went to a different place (the upper region of Hades) than where they go now since his resurrection (paradise, the third Heaven). In the same way, the souls of the righteous reside in a different place now, prior to Judgement Day, than where they will dwell after the Judgement Day. Catholics prefer to refer to this place as purgatory, where God completes the purifying work after a person's life on earth basically have been oriented toward God and his will. Purgatory is not a second chance for salvation for those who have rejected God or lived evil lives. Neither is it a safety net for people who hope God will overlook serious sin in their lives if they die unrepentant. The early Christians believed that the Holy Spirit had led them to pray for the dead based on this understanding of man's destiny after death. The early Christians believed that their prayers could hasten God's work of purifying and urging their deceased relatives and friends from sin by calling upon his mercy.

The doctrine of purgatory is related to Isaiah's vision of God on a throne with the angels surrounding him crying, "Holy, holy, holy is the Lord of host" (Is 6:1-3) Isaiah's immediate response was: "Woe is me! For I am a man of unclean lips…yet my eyes have seen the Lord of hosts!" But the Lord sent an angel to purify Isaiah's lips with a burning coal from the altar of God and touched his mouth and said, "Behold, this has touched your lips, your guilt is taken away and your sin forgiven." (Is 6:7) Only then was Isaiah able to speak the Word of God to the people.

When people come before God in reality (not just in a vision), they will see their sin as it really is, ugly and detestable and cry out, "Woe is me!" and this is how we came to believe that a purification by fire—a purgatory—would come upon those Christians whose lives and works were imperfect in God's sight, although they themselves would be saved. The image of fire connected with purgatory shows that it is painful, yet also cleansing and purifying. Even though we are saved, if a person dies in some bondage to sin, or has been crippled by sin's effects, this sin and its effects must be removed, forgiven, and purged before the person sees God face-to-face because of God's holiness.

God even turned away from Jesus for a while, as I understand it, when Jesus carried the weight of all of our sins on the cross causing him to say, "Father, why have you forsaken me?" Jesus felt disconnected from his Heavenly father when his father turned away unable to look at sin since no sin can stand before him, in the Holy of Holies.

Even after being saved we must still follow his ways, his laws and his commandments. Believe it or not most, if not all, *can't* do it alone. But again, God makes it so simple for us to follow. Surrender to him all areas of our lives you can't control and he will lead us. What more could we ask? The more we surrender, the more he is happy to assist us and the more we will want to surrender. Why not just surrender our whole self to him from the beginning then we can't go wrong. Using this concept, my life is getting so easy to live and so uncomplicated that I'm still baffled and in awe every day. If he did it for me, he will do it for you.

After the Judgement Day, the new Heaven will be created as detailed in Revelations, the New Jerusalem with streets paved with gold and no one wanting for anything.

Our reborn Spirit already exists in us after we are saved in the same manner that it will exists after our body dies. Our Spirits already inhabit the dimension we will be fully translated upon death and we will be more conscious of our Spirits in Heaven. Now our souls are comprised of

our thought, emotions, willpower and consciousness.
Our awareness of the world around us, as well as our
inner selves, comes from the soul. The good news is our
personalities will be refined like gold but who we are
before we die is who we will be after. So our soul/spirits
will remain intact and essentially the same after this
purification process. However, we will possess new
heavenly bodies more appropriate to our new environment.
Death is a changed existence which is extended, not
exterminated minus all the wrongs, distortions, wounding
or bondage of this life. We will retain our original
God-given personality and character when we rise from
the dead. Everyone will live after death—either in eternal
death (separation from God and His life) or eternal life
in Heaven—and so will all exist forever. With God or
without Him.

In keeping our own personalities, we will be able to
know and recognize everyone in Heaven. We will be as
distinctive as we had been on earth. (Just as the Apostles
immediately recognized Moses and Elijah in the garden
as they were talking to Jesus, even though they had been
gone for hundreds of years prior, we will recognize each
other.) Imagine meeting that child you lost in the womb
or your spouse or all the relatives you've always wanted
to know whom you felt left us prematurely. No, we
will not relate to each other or live as our earthly family
re-united with soul mates to live as eternity, but we
will recognize each other. We do not become wisps of
air—one with the universe—as some would like us to
believe. We will be ageless and changeless. No one will
be conceived in Heaven because the finite number of
people will have already been achieved.

Grief, anguish, sadness, hurts, sickness, anxiety are things of this life which produce groans from the depths of our hearts will be completely absent in Heaven. Nothing will affect us or oppress us. We will have no mood swings, since Heaven is the fullest expression of God's will and way, we should expect it to satisfy us as nothing else can.

Also we will not need an address to find our home. The moment we see it, we will know it is ours because it will be exactly what our soul always wanted. But best of all we will be in God's presence for eternity and all that is evil will be locked up and can never touch us again.

Now imagine you just won the lottery and can't wait to tell everyone of your good fortune. Imagine that cute thing your child did and you run to tell your relatives and friends. Imagine receiving an interesting e-mail or hearing a good joke you can't wait to share. Imagine finding the deal or your life while out shopping and you phone to tell your best friend. Imagine holding-in this huge secret and feeling you will bust open if you don't tell everyone you know right now. I just can't imagine holding back everything I know right now.

I want everyone I know to share in this ever lasting life with our God. You can also let anyone else you choose in on this Good News. This fleeting moment in time, in our current physical state, is nothing compared to what awaits us.

Now, go take on the Day!

Personal Salvation—It's not just for those other Christians

As Catholics, we believe Salvation was made possible by Jesus Christ who died on the cross. This concept is taught, talked about, around and through, but the idea of personal salvation is avoided and/or under emphasized. We are told to believe abstract principles and accept salvation through faith that it will happen. And it may, I don't think anyone can say with absolute certainty one way or the other. But, waiting and wondering and hoping whether our faith is strong enough or our lives are good enough or prayers loud enough or long enough to reach Heaven is an unnecessary gamble.

What a tremendous peace of mind one receives after personal Salvation when you then know in your heart as your Spirit is reconnected with God that you are going to Heaven with absolute certainty. And during the Rapture, when Jesus comes for us we will be in that first wave of saved souls that he will shepherd back to his father's house in a room he already has prepared for us. His feelings for us are quite explicit. (John 17)

To become a Christian doesn't mean to accept a philosophy, or a set of rules, or to believe a list of abstract principles. To become a Christian means to have God come and live in us (Col 1:27). It's as easy as just asking him:

Repent: Admit you're a sinner.

Convert: Your life to follow Jesus and his ways.

Be Forgiven: Have sins taken away and records swept clean.

To live forgiven and be born again.

—(John 3:1-21)

51

Salvation is a little, itty-bitty word, until it happens to you. Then you have your first experience of Christian Life because during salvation we experience the incoming of the Holy Spirit. Any one denomination will not get you to Heaven, only your personal salvation can.

Catholicism is the largest Christian denomination in the world. When personal salvation does happen, the Catholic Church as a whole doesn't know what to do with us. We are full of this newfound outpouring of God's presence and love within us.

Unfortunately many are drawn away to other Christian Churches to try to make sense of what is happening to them. I've learned the second largest Christian group in the world is comprised of ex-Catholics. Some are drawn to the charismatic movement, where available, to seek the fellowship of other understanding souls. Yet others quietly serve their own churches with a new zeal for the various ministries. Others still, meet outside the church in prayer groups, coed groups or out in their community, to live the lives we were meant to live. There are many scriptural references to this praise, worship and prayer in groups outside of the church! There are not nearly enough clergy to go around so it is a good way to keep us accountable to each other.

The real presence of Jesus in the Tabernacle is so strong to me at times, it floors me as I drop to my knees and bask in his love and companionship. So if anything, having a personal relationship has helped me appreciate and understand the scriptures at levels I never knew possible. The sacraments have taken on a new and deeper meaning in my life. Heaven is the state of perfect fellowship with God and one another. And we can have a foretaste of it here and now! We become God's beloved children!

Catholic Christians, since the time of Christ, have had all this information. They possess all the ways and means and have all the traditions of praising God and accepting him. The genius of Catholicism is that it never throws anything away. How sad that so many Catholics run to the religions of the East and to New Age to find embodied practices of prayer when we have them in such abundance in our own ecclesial attic!

(For example: Meditate on the Sorrowful Mysteries of the Rosary, the Agony in the Garden, the Scourging, the Crowned with thorns, etc., which as a discipline puts us into a mystical frame of mind. Use it as a mantra to dull and quiet the mind.)

Accepting Jesus into our lives personally can happen at confirmation, but like so many things it becomes a formal action with no real results expected. Although from time to time, acceptance may come through confirmation.

Could it be that by keeping us in the dark about this the Catholic Hierarchy feel we will not be held personally responsible for not knowing? Does anyone know for sure? Why take that chance?

As Catholics, we also have our Blessed Mother Mary and our devotion, respect and esteem for her and the role she plays as the co-redemptress in God's plan of salvation.

But yet we leave the part of personal salvation to groups gathered mainly outside of the Catholic Church. Many argue personal salvation is the greatest miracle performed in modern time. The Catholic Church teaches it is the conversion of the bread and wine into the body and blood of Christ. Our disagreements about specific doctrines should be overshadowed by our primary purpose in life to know, love and serve Jesus Christ!

Most other Christian denominations have taken this basic idea of personal salvation from the original church and ran with it, along with the knowledge of knowing the reality of God within them. Too bad they did not accept Mary or the Sacraments for the total package. Perhaps we can borrow back the idea of personal salvation from them. Cardinal Terence Cooke has said, "Next to zeal for God's Glory, zeal for our own holiness, our own personal salvation is our first and greatest duty." In James (1:5) "If you really want to know what God wants you to do, simply ask him and he will gladly tell you." We must believe that God speaks or reveals his plan in such a way that we can hear it and follow it. There are some who believe that God has only revealed the skeletal outline of that plan through the Bible and the teachings of our church. There are others who believe that revelation ceased with the death of the last apostle. Unknowing Christians cling to the Hebrews verse that says "He died for our sins once and for all and as Catholics we should not be joining in the holy sacrifice of the mass."

Well much like a movie or a play, actors don't die over and over. They are recreating the story each and every time. As Catholics, we do not kill Jesus Christ over and over sacrificing him every time we come together. We recreate the events "in memory of Him" and during the consecration of the host, we have a memorial of what he did for us as we all come together as a church to sacrifice ourselves and our sins—to unite with Christ.

The second experience after salvation is receiving, or making welcome the Holy Spirit so Jesus can pour out this new life from our spirits. And to baptize our body and souls with refreshing and renewing power. Our minds come alive in a new way to God's reality. References to this Baptism of the Holy Spirit are found in just about all the Gospels. (John 1:33, Acts 1:5, Matt 3:11, Mark 1:8, Luke 3:16)

If you are a Catholic Christian, by reading this you are aware of this plan and will be held personally responsible for accepting Jesus into your life with a simple prayer that must come from the heart. Remember, God does know the intentions of our heart. The Sinner's prayer is also known as the, "Prayer of Commitment." This prayer was found in a Franciscan prayer book and is available in many other prayer books.

The Sinners Prayer

Jesus, I repent of my sins. I renounce the evil one and all his works. I surrender my life to you and I truly accept you as the Son of the Living God. I receive you now into my life as my personal Lord and Savior. Fill me with your Holy Spirit. I love you, Jesus.

Thank You Jesus!

God's promises to us are very explicit in "The Catholic Living Bible" (John 17) and the plan for Salvation is in Romans in order (5:8, 5:12, 6:23, 10:9-13, 10:17) Also known as the Roman Road as well as having our name written in Lamb's book of life (Rev 21:27).

Too Bad Most Catholics expect nothing and that's usually what they get!

When we pray this prayer, we may actually feel something happen, or we may not. Our "spirit" which comes alive through Jesus Christ is in a place far deeper than our emotions, therefore sometimes there will be an emotional reaction, and sometimes not.

We will find that we are different because Jesus will do what He has promised. But, this is only the beginning, and even though this newly connected spirit within us is willing, the body is weak and very susceptible to outside forces and distractions.

The great saints we have all heard about or read about started out as we have as ordinary people. Then, after their salvation and baptism of the Holy Spirit opened themselves wide to receive the goodness of God. They waited and listened for God to reveal his purpose, his plan for their lives. They readily accepted being God's beloved children.

Summary

As I was led to write these pages, please keep in mind, it only skims the surface of all there is to know for myself as well as for others. If nothing else, this has peaked my curiosity, which began with my salvation some three months ago. I hope it has stirred your curiosity to continue seeking and searching for yourselves. None of us will ever know all there is to know in this lifetime and doesn't hurt to get a head start on the next.

A Word of advice—"The Sinners Prayer" mentioned earlier—Say it like you mean it and everything you seek and read will make so much more sense as the Holy Spirit will lead you and guide you and reveal things to you in ways you would have never dreamed possible. This is just one of my examples: While reading in book of Acts, I suddenly received this enlightenment of the work of God that startled me so much I didn't know whether to laugh or cry. The Jewish high priests that wanted Jesus dead and out of their way to prevent the message from being spread any further were actually used by God to help spread the Word and I'm sure they never even knew what hit them! They summoned their generals, including Saul, (because they had their own armies back then) to eradicate Christianity from the face of the earth. So they set about arresting, beating and killing them with a vengeance. Poor Saint Steven had the dubious role of becoming the first Christian martyr.

All this while the Apostles and the other 110 or so people that were with Jesus in the upper room during the first Pentecost were given direction to spread the Word to the ends of the earth. Not understanding the real message, the

ends of the earth for them meant the Israeli border and
they stopped there. But along comes Saul and their troops
and force them out of Israel as they fled spreading the
Word along the way (I can just picture them yelping all
the way like puppies). Once this task was accomplished
and fire was lit under their behinds, courtesy of the Jewish
High Priest, God took Saul aside and blinded him and
asked why he had been persecuting him. Saul was at a
loss for Words, he did not understand since he was being
a good soldier and followed orders without questioning
his superiors. He sent him into town and told him to
wait there till he sent a messenger, which happened to
be Ananias to pray over him and that's when he saw the
light. After that, Saul used that same vengeance and
determination to spread the Word being the loyal and
faithful servant that he was. In addition, the apostles
never knew what the reason for that motivation was that
they saw as persecution. There are so many ways God
is working in our lives right now we might never
understand in this life. Too bad our Jewish friends don't
see it this way, perhaps we can enlighten some of them.

Jesus also admonished the apostles when they questioned
him for talking to the Samaritan woman at the well in
(John 4). Since she did not worship in the same type of
temple they did. He told them it did not matter where
you worship so much as how you worship. I'm starting to
find this out as I visit different Christian churches but it
should come as no surprise since we are all connected to
the same Holy Spirit. The ideas, thoughts, understanding
and interpretation of Scripture are all guided by him and I
use the teachings from these other sources to supplement
my knowledge of Christianity.

Become like a child and accept his grace without question. What he did was so awesome it defies words. Pretend that you are in a foreign land with your own father and you knowingly commit a crime. You are sent to Jail and sentenced to death. The laws of that land are just, but very harsh and demand death for the crime committed. Your father comes to visit you as you confess to him what you did was stupid and wrong and are truly repentant for what you did. Your father believes you and can see it in your heart through your eyes. He then steps in to accept the punishment in your place so that your crimes/sins may be absolved and you may live.

This is simply what our God did for us. Deal with it!

Part III

60

Abortion

How important is the value of human life? Life was exceedingly cheap prior to Christ's coming, even expendable. In ancient times, a child sacrifice was common among the Canaanites. The prophets of Baal commonly practiced child sacrifices. It was dangerous for a baby to be conceived in classical Rome or Greece where abortion was rampant. Abandonment was commonplace. Sick, unwanted or deformed infants were routinely taken into the forest to be consumed by wild animals or to starve. Worse yet, female infants were abandoned more often because they were considered inferior. If that was not enough, the two thirds that did survive were considered the property of their father and he would kill them at a whim or sell them as slaves. Only half the children born would live past the age of eight. Christianity bridged the gap between the Jews—who first received the divine revelation that man was made in God's image and the pagans who attributed little value to human life.

Note: Baal was that nasty Idol of a god that kept surfacing in the Old Testament and side tracking the Jews into worshipping him instead. Fortunately today's modern society this does not happen, or does it? Has Baal now been replaced by our desire for material things of this world. The evil one is very clever and his biggest deceit is convincing so many that he does not exist. He is distracting us in so many ways that take our mind off God.

Before I formed you in the womb I knew you.

—(Jer 1:5)

He thought about us and planned us and has a purpose in mind for us. God knew us before we were born and created in His image (the image of His spirit). The circumstances that brought us into the world do not matter. God chose us to come into being for a purpose. Christians cherish life as sacred, even the life of the unborn child. This is what Christians understand and that is why the Catholics have denounced abortions and any form of contraception because it would be interfering with God's will for us. Many Christian denominations have succumbed to accepting abortion and other forms of contraception. They are changing with the times and prevailing attitudes of the people who are being led by non-Christian sources. But God never changes and his Word is always the same and always will be. The Catholic Church is one of the few that have stood by this teaching and not given in.

The Ten Commandments are the foundation for the laws of our land. Do not kill, steal, lie, commit adultery, etc. America has lost its way and we are forced to vote on whether abortion is right or wrong, confronting the increasing claims against the validity of the Bible as being inspired by God. Sometimes laws are interpreted using tainted logic. And laws making abortion legal or making it ok to steal, lie and commit adultery a re overlooked. Responsibility for one's actions are becoming more of a civil rights issue, while remaining morally wrong. We all know who the ultimate judge will be on these matters. God's laws will never be superceded by an earthly judge's interpretation.

Ultimately, I suppose it is a woman's right to choose. After all, we were created with a free will to choose

God and his laws or not. Each individual will answer to our maker for his or her actions in the courtroom that counts.

Mother Theresa of Calcutta stunned and silenced the country's political and religious leaders assembled in Washington D.C. for the national Prayer Breakfast in 1994 with her simple yet profound and direct message saying, "I feel that the greatest destroyer of peace today is abortion because it is a war against the child, a direct killing of the innocent child, murdered by the mother herself. And if we accept that a mother can kill even her own child, how can we tell other people not to kill one another? By abortion, the mother does not learn to love, but kills even her own child to solve her problems. And by abortion, the father is told that he does not have to take any responsibility at all for the child he has brought into the world. That father is likely to put other women into the same trouble. So abortion just leads to more abortion. Any country that accepts abortion is not teaching the people to love, but to use any violence to get what they want. Please don't kill the child. I want the child. Please give me the child. I am willing to accept any child who would be aborted, and to give that child to a married couple who will love the child, and be loved by the child."

Is there a more repulsive notion than the term, "unwanted child?" I often wonder what our children and future generations will think of us, a society with lavish material resources, yet poor in spirit when it comes to making room for a fetus (Latin for "little one"). It almost seems America is afraid of defenseless little babies. We have the most liberal abortion laws in the entire world, and it's legal, for *any* reason through all nine months of the pregnancy in the United States to terminate life. All this while there are more than two million couples on waiting lists longing to adopt!

Psychiatrists are astounded to find that when their patients are injected with truth serum and they regress to their womb, they start crying out to God as they once knew him there.

Numerous women have told me a fascinating story about their newborn babies. It seems that when they held their child, they started speaking to them about God and angels. The babies would smile and laugh as if they were acknowledging and understood. One woman told me a story of her two-year-old grandson who kept insisting that his parents leave him alone with his newborn baby sister for a few minutes because he needed to talk to her. They of course were very hesitant as to what his motives were, but after a week or so they relented and left him alone with the door slightly ajar to observe. He started asking his sister if she remembered the angels and God because he was starting to forget and wanted to know if they were O.K.

His parents were astounded and sought some explanation from their priest. His best reply was that children from the moment of conception are assigned a guardian angel and have a full knowledge of God and will retain this knowledge for a while, especially if they are constantly reminded from birth. How many more souls would become most holy if properly guided from the very start.

Could this be true? Where in the scripture is this supported? I came across the answer in Isaiah 46. "Listen to me...you whom I have upheld since you were conceived, and have carried since your birth." It reaffirmed to me that our Lord is with us from the moment of conception.

I thought about this for a few days when I suddenly was led to a new understanding of this newfound knowledge. From the moment of conception we enjoy an intimate personal relationship with God and are aware of his existence in a very real way.

Sometime after our birth or after the loss of our childhood innocence and/or the result of original sin, we lose touch with that knowledge. We start to have a sense of emptiness, a longing for something and we can't quite put a finger on it. We have this hunger we can't identify because our mother's womb is such a distant memory and we try to fill that void with relationships, toys, homes, cars, jobs, vacations, drugs, etc. Some of these objects fill our desires for an hour, a week or a year, but then we start longing again in an attempt to find ourselves and fill that emptiness inside. The whole time we are unable to identify that longing as a spiritual hunger, a void that only God can fill. We enjoyed a spiritual connection in our mother's womb, which for some of us remains a distant memory lost deep in our subconscious. It's difficult to pinpoint the origin of what it is we are seeking and longing for. We know that feeling of inner peace, joy and happiness which came so naturally in the womb because of our personal relationship with God. It's an experience we spend the rest of our lives seeking to know once again.

God is the source of that inner peace, joy and happiness. Those are just natural by-products of being drawn closer to God. He will re-establish that link and we will be born again with the knowledge of God's unconditional love for us. It's as simple as asking Him. Acknowledging Him, and asking forgiveness for sins that have already been bought and paid for by his first born son, Jesus the redeemer. We are his beloved children, the redeemed, and there is nothing he will not do for us.

No wonder we come out into this world kicking and screaming!

Saints

Saints are people who have been chosen as holy to God, but foremost, humans that were touched by a dedication and zeal to holiness not known to many. Sure, they expressed anger, had their bad days and a lot of good ones. They did not keep all the rules and remain blameless. They lived in a real world, going out and loving the real people whom God has put into their lives.

In the early church anyone who gave his life for Christ or was open to have the Spirit work through them became a saint and there are probably over 10,000 of them. Today becoming a saint is as bureaucratic as passing a law through Congress and the support of a country of origin. One needs to go through the steps of beautification and canonization to become one and wait years or decades to be officially recognized. Truth is, there are hundreds, perhaps thousands of ordinary people today doing extraordinary things in the name of Christ with no recognition, as should be because all is done with the glory of God and not for personal gain or satisfaction or pride. God's grace and mercy is not just poured out on pre-qualified do-gooders and regular church attendees. God qualifies the called and gives us the necessary talents, gifts and desire to serve him. We should all be striving for sainthood without earthly recognition. To die to oneself and become less, doing our part and staying in the background. God calls us, then qualifies us no matter what stage in life we are in or what we may have done.

Prayer seems to be a normal way for saints on earth to support each other. Catholics believe that if we ask our fellow saints on earth to pray for us, we should also be able to ask for prayers from the saints who are already united with the Lord. If the prayers of certain Christians here on earth seem to have special power because of their great faith or holiness, how much more powerful and effective are the prayers of those who are fully united to God in Heaven! Now, St. Augustine warned against any devotion to the saints becoming a form of worship and the saints themselves forbid anyone to offer them the worship they know is reserved for God, as is clear in the case of Paul and Barnabas (Acts 14:8). More importantly, we should use the lives of the saints to reflect on their examples of living the life of faith. Sometimes the most unlikely people make this list, such as:

Saul of Tarsus who killed hundreds of Christians before his own conversion.

St Longinus, the guard present at the crucifixion, who when piercing the side of Christ was subsequently healed of a malady of his eyes when the blood of Jesus flowed down his lance and he rubbed his eyes with it. At his own execution for not renouncing Christ, he told the near blind governor that upon his death his eyesight would be restored and it was, spurring his conversion of the governor!

St Elizabeth Seton opened the first free Catholic Schools in New York City, thus planting a seed for the American parochial education.

St Eramus also known as St Elmo often is invoked by sailors through stormy waters. Often during a thunder and lightning storm at sea, a bluish electrical tinge can be seen around the masthead, (St. Elmo's Fire) a signal sailors anxiously look for to signify that their ship has been taken under his protection. This bishop's legend comes from a sermon he completed during a fierce storm where lightning bolts that shook the ground kept landing near his feet.

Once we see their human side and struggles, we may find we have more in common with them than we thought. We are to live in Christ in whatever state of life to which we are called and are enabled to do by divine grace, freely given to every individual. The one common denominator I've seen in all the lives of saints is their dedication to fervent daily prayer. Their holiness attained by a complete submission to the will of God.

Books on the lives of saints are plentiful and their lives should be studied, not so we pray to them, but to obtain a better insight on how to draw closer to God, by following their example.

Angels

I believe my favorite, all time angel story comes from the book on Padre Pio. It seems his aide would like to sleep as long as possible before attending to Padre Pio. In the early morning hours, he would get a knock on the door and a voice calling to him to wake up. He assumed it was Padre Pio, but when he would go into the church he'd find the good Padre finishing up a service or a confessional session.

He questioned Padre Pio one day on this and wondered who was stopping by to wake him every day at the same time. Padre replied, "I wish you would go out and get an alarm clock because I'm getting tired of sending my Guardian Angel to wake you every morning!"

It's true Padre Pio had a remarkable relationship with his guardian whom he would affectionately call, "his little companion of infancy whom he invited every morning to sing praises with him to the delight of their hearts."

That started me thinking of the connection to ourselves as children growing up with imaginary friends? Were they really so imaginary or is it because of the child like innocence we were, in fact, connecting with our own, "Little Companions of Infancy." I don't believe it is a just a coincidence the children who seem to need their angels have these 'friends.' Parents do need to show caution and discern the source and messages received by their child since the great deceiver is capable of mimicking all. The Bible says in (Psalm 91:11), "He will give his angels charge of you, to guard you in all your ways." How sad that we lose sight of this invaluable resource provided by our God.

While I don't profess to know but a miniscule fraction about angels as some other great theologians, I would have to say Padre Pio's angel was probably a good candidate for their perception of "Sainthood." He worked him constantly and his angel had to provide him round the clock protection from unseen negative spiritual forces that continually haunted him.

My understanding is that Angels were created by God during the second day of creation. The full compliment of angels were created then and none have been created since.

There is a hierarchy among them as follows:

Seraphim—closest to God and continually singing praises to God with six wings

Cherubim—depicted as bizarre winged animals to chubby little winged children

Dominion—oldest looking of angels and supervisors to angels below them

Virtues—ones who work miracles on Earth and Guardian Angels

Powers—bad cops of Angels, they come down on evil and keep demons and devils and evil spirits at bay

Principalities—protect cities, nations and leaders of religious faiths.

Archangels—messenger angels delivering God's decrees to the people

Angels—work most closely with us ordinary humans.

Their main duties are as messengers of God and that of protecting God's chosen ones. Books that get into more detail are readily available in libraries and bookstores.

What strikes me the most is how many more books and movies are available on witchcraft, possessions, demonic activity and the occult. People have no problem relating to this and believing in it as being a real threat. They are and they should not be tampered with or entertained.

Too bad the majority of these same people have a problem relating to or believing in the good spiritual forces around us or that we can also open ourselves to be possessed by the Holy Spirit of God.

The Lord's Prayer

In (Luke 11:1), one of Jesus' disciples asked him, "Lord, teach us how to pray." And Jesus answered, "Pray in this manner." He was giving us an example of how to really pray to our Father and not just how to say the 'Our Father.' Of course, for Catholics, this prayer has a special place in communal worshiping or when meditating with the rosary. But in our own personal prayer life, we should learn to pray using this as a guideline.

Our Father who art in Heaven, hallowed be thy name...

1. This is the first part in which we need to praise and worship our God in all things, even in our infirmities and know he will use all things for good for those that trust and believe in him. Praising God takes us out of self and puts us into God. Therefore a significant amount of time should be spent here. If we have a real problem with this concept, *Get used to it! Get over it!* Because if you don't, you're going to have a nervous breakdown in Heaven where the majority of our time will be spent doing this.

Thy Kingdom come, thy will be done...

2. Seek his plan. He has a plan for our lives and wants to reveal it step by step, moment by moment. God is speaking to his children all the time and we need to quiet our minds and listen. We need to tune our minds for an answer, his insight which may come in external signs and symbols, people, events, scripture and church, but primarily internally through our thoughts and

deepest intuition and sometimes in dreams and visions. I believe if he were to reveal his plan for our lives right up front, many of us would run away screaming and saying, "No way God," "Are you kidding," "You've got the wrong person." But as we seek his plan he will gradually, passively transform us to accomplish his ultimate plan in a most painless manner.

Give Us this day our Daily Bread/Grace...

3. We must learn to rely on his divine providence. God wishes to provide for all our needs, spiritual and physical. This is the promise of the covenant. God provides, 'Ask and you Shall Receive.' The more we open up, yield and simply allow ourselves to be drawn deeply into the Lord's love, the more our lives will be directed and come into alignment with God's will. We allow the Holy Spirit to work out his meaning in our lives.

Forgive us our trespasses as we forgive those who trespass against us...

4. This is such an explosive, yet underrated statement. While it is true that Christ came to pay the price for our sins, his intention was to free us from all pain, guilt, anger, bitterness, resentment, worries and frustration. No, we don't have to offer them up or have to carry our cross as some of us have been taught. All these things are not of God and they only serve to keep our focus away from him, to keep us distracted. We need to surrender all these things to him as well. We all live lives burdened with these afflictions and psychologists have no answer for

them. What they do tell us, however, is that most people handle them using one or more of these four mechanisms: repression, denial, rationalization and projection. But it doesn't go away. Forgiveness is the only practical, powerful, foolproof answer.

Lead us not into temptation, but deliver us from evil.

5. Dear Lord, tell us where not to go, what not to do or say. Intervene for us. God is our protector. He warns us of impending evil, spiritually from sin; emotionally from worldly depression and fear; and physically from any danger. We have to learn how to hear His voice so that we will heed His warnings.

We pay a heavy price for not listening.

Relationships

The more I get into the Bible the more I see that everything we need to lead the life God wants for us is right there, in black and white.

Relationships are the main focus in Ephesians that caught my eye. Paul is trying to convey to his friends the type of lives they should lead. He explains how being single is a valid, noble style of living, a holy calling. It is a gift for this time we have now and Matthew (Matt: 22) concurs by saying we will all be single in Heaven, like Angels. When Christ is our focus he completes us. People can enhance or compliment each other, but not complete the way a relationship with God can. A single person is concerned with the affairs of the Lord in this divine opportunity and should be content where he/she is at this point in time in a loving relationship with our Maker, the one who loves us most. Contentment and fulfillment are not found in another person, but in a loving relationship with our maker. When and if we get to the point in life where we feel we need a mate, don't rush into it, just pray and know God is probably working on a person for us right now. We don't have to settle but should maintain our noble standard of self-control. We can still be healthy individuals without having to express ourselves sexually to anyone. Being lonely and single is one thing, but being lonely and married is another kind of hurtful, destructive loneliness. St. Paul also goes on to say that it is better then, to be married than have lustful experiences or thoughts. Be warned though that marriage and children will never fix anything, it is not a means to an end since contentment and fulfillment are not found in another person.

Marriage, of course, is another type of noble calling and with it responsibilities change as do affairs and freedoms with the concern of the family and spouse. Marriage should be rooted in faith. Faith that gives couples energy for daily lives and strength for hard times plus a vision of what they are called to become. In searching for someone, women should guard their heart and make wise decisions. They need to make the most of every opportunity and not become vulnerable. Maintaining a spiritual integrity will foster a healthy relationship. Men should keep women pure and there must not even be a hint of sexual immorality. God's original intent for marriage was to be a good, positive thing. When he looked at Adam, he said it wasn't good for him to be alone, so he created woman and told them to become one, be fruitful and multiply. Satan does not like anything good and does what he can to disrupt this union."Woman submit to your Man" taken out of context sounds very chauvinistic but when the time is taken to read the whole account we learn something quite different. There should be a Christ centered mutual submission to one another in love, honor and respect. If there is no love, please respect and honor each other especially while dating and keep the woman pure.

A survey conducted by a national magazine on sexuality found them not only overwhelmed by the response (over 100,000 returns) but also by the outcome. Prostitutes, not surprisingly, are left with an empty feeling and loneliness after a trick. Sexually promiscuous women did feel a high after the initial encounter but that feeling quickly waned. In an unloving marriage where Christ is not the center of a relationship women still felt emptiness and more a sense of obligation to the act. The real shocker came when Christian women responded from a Christ centered relationship because they were by far the most sexually fulfilled and content women who took the survey.

We bring a lot of turmoil into our own lives. When God's laws for us are followed and everything is done in his time, everything just seems to come together. When there is a violation of these laws and rules from God, things eventually go awry. He loves us so much and wants the best for his people. When will we all learn?

Divorce Group Meeting

I remained fairly quiet during our initial meeting listening to all of our stories and to my amazement found that I could relate to almost all of them. One woman brought in a bag full of books she had read to try and make sense of everything. I also have a collection, I'm almost embarrassed to say, that would rival hers on topics ranging from co-dependency, addictions, boundaries, birth order books, enabling as well as assorted titles from mars, venus and other psycho babble literature. I had to find an answer as to what went wrong and I was approaching it from every angle I could. A certain level of understanding is good to have and may help us get through the rough time as we sit and lick our wounds.

Interestingly enough the vast majority of women in the group were in the health care profession. These are classic examples of co-dependents and caretakers, since these are practically prerequisites for such professions. When those enabling, care taking traits start to become skewed too far in one direction in our personal relationships with a dependent, needy person who is practically unable to give love and only take, something eventually gives. That person we thought we knew starts sensing an empty feeling or a need for some more excitement and before long they start to look outside the home to feel good, to be happy which they have convinced themselves they deserve and can only find elsewhere. But, it's probably just me speaking.

Another person in the group mentioned she took drugs to overcome her despair, loneliness, rejection and I was right in the thick of that myself. (After a particular lively scenario between my ex and myself, I told my eldest daughter to take her sisters and leave for a while. She looked me right in the eye and said, "Dad, it's not just mom anymore.") Those words were like daggers, they really hit home. I, the provider, the protector of my home was losing control of the situation and myself. I had allowed myself to be dragged down to a new low. I sought help and started taking Prozac, Ambien (sleeping pill) and Lorazapam (for anxiety) in addition to the Axid I had started taking months earlier for acid reflux.

Now drugs are good and necessary in some cases and can help us get through the confusion and despair as we try to regain our senses. A co-worker knew of my situation and offered to listen if I ever needed to talk. He also told me his story, how he was still bitter three years later and still on anti-depressants (which he expected to be taking the rest of his life so he would not have to feel the hurt and pain). All I could think about after that encounter was "Thank you Jesus for showing me a good example of how I don't want to wind up."

Another woman spoke of anger and resentment years after her separation and she said fortunately she did not own a weapon because she would have been tempted to use it. I found myself there also. One day after my ex had already moved out of the house and was acting out in what I perceived to be self-destructive behavior while my youngest was visiting with her. I had nowhere to go and was powerless to intervene.

The same thing happened to me that happened to that woman who said she felt a calmness and inner peace in church one day that changed her outlook on her situation. I fell to my knees and said, "God, I can't take it anymore, help me and take away the pain." A sudden feeling of tranquility and inner peace swept over me. I got up from the floor and went to bed and had the best night of sleep I have had in months. It wasn't until a few days later that I came to realize what happened that night. I asked God for help and received it in a most dramatic fashion. I've never recognized a prayer actually being answered before.

That sense of inner peace, joy and happiness has only gotten deeper ever since that night. A few weeks ago I discovered these are only natural by-products of growing closer to God, and it was just as simple as asking him. But, it's probably just me speaking.

I could have spent the rest of my life searching for answers in books or in lifelong sessions with psychologists or group sessions and never found any. I could have stayed with medications and numbed myself as my co-worker has done. I could have made myself crazier and took matters into my own hands, but instead have come to a better place in life.

I don't need to tell the people in the group this has been the most excruciating, gut wrenching experience I have ever gone through. I have experienced the death of two sisters and my dad some twenty-five years ago, but there was mourning and closure after some time. But now a part of us is gone and we can't really mourn that loss and have the same type of closure.

My spouse and I grew apart, I stopped growing, too busy taking care of everything and everyone except myself. My spouse grew in a whole new direction. Not necessarily better, or healthier direction, but a new direction. The ones left behind are the ones hurt the most. They attend meetings and try to make sense of it all. I've accepted it was not a rejection of me personally. She just went in a different direction still searching to fill that void which she has not identified. An emptiness and a longing for true happiness which she will not find externally or with anyone else.

Initially this was a tough time in my life, but I would go through it again with the knowledge of where it has led me. I now know God is controlling everything and working out all things that happen for good. All we have to do is trust in him. I have found inner peace, joy and happiness in having a personal relationship with God. I also realize ultimately we really are only responsible for ourselves.

My church attendance prior to our problems had dwindled to the point where I was only going on the holy days of obligation, which in my book were reduced to Christmas and Easter. I was a like a lost sheep out in the pasture, but God found me, he called me by name and I now realize he has a plan and purpose for me. He was standing there all along, not wanting to force himself on me, but waiting patiently for me to seek him out. His Prodigal son.

> "Man (his soul) is restless until he finds God" ·
> —St. Augustine.

Inner Healing

In psychology we learn there are three levels of every human mind: The conscious, which is engaged with whatever we are doing and thinking at any given moment. The subconscious is where we keep record of birth dates, anniversaries, names, multiplication tables, etc. These facts and memories are available for use whenever we want to recall them. Then there is the unconscious mind where information began being stored from conception to just prior to our active memory, which usually begins about the age three to five. Here also lie hidden things we don't want to face or live with which is why this is also referred to as the cellar of the mind. We develop coping mechanisms that are our defenses and form shields around us. They are developed to prevent us from being overwhelmed by situations in life that may at the time be out of our control, especially as children. These defenses are also intended to spare us from honest confrontation with ourselves. This "other" material consists of memory that has been effectively repressed, rationalized or denied out of existence.

What we have stored in our unconscious mind is not dead however, but buried alive. These hidden events, feelings, reactions and prejudices continue to haunt, bother and to influence us. Since we are not consciously aware of these hidden memories, we are not aware of their impact on our thoughts, actions and reactions.

These memories can just as easily manifest themselves in physical ailments such as arthritis, diabetes, back problems and even some forms of cancer. Studies show trauma depresses the immune system and cancer can

begin to form in our bodies. Fr. Robert DeGrandis, a
very spirit filled priest with many books on healing, has
even gone as far as to say that upwards of 60% of illness
and disease can be traced back to a root cause in our
hidden memory. Buried resentments, anger, fears,
unforgiveness as well as lack of affirmation may be
the root cause of many physical ailments. This root cause is
where the healing process must begin. A good psychiatrist,
psychologist or counselor can certainly help, especially in
extreme cases, but generally speaking years of visits and
thousands of dollars can be avoided if we initially place
ours ills in the hands of the great healer, our God.

"Confession is good for the soul." These are very
powerful Words and a very good place to start for the
inner healing of painful memories. A good cleansing
confession where we pray and meditate for a complete
confession. Forgiveness is the key and the forgiveness
prayer is a good place to start. (Eph 5:6) Our Lord
is calling us out of darkness and into joy. We can
understand how God has put us together to live a
full life the way it was meant to be.

Another good way to understand this connection in
the healing process is to examine how we were created.
We were created so that our spiritual, physical and
psychological parts work in harmony. When any one
of the three are hurting, one or both of the others
will suffer.

Prayer should be at the center of our lives. When we are
hurting and don't know how to pray or talk to God at
a personal level, we should seek out a good minister,
prayer group or someone in the healing ministry that will

pray with us in asking God for guidance. Someone who is very open to being used by the Holy Spirit in Word gifts is especially helpful. Word gifts are, as I understand them, recognizing the voice of God within us. The closer and deeper I get to the Holy Spirit, I am beginning to realize I have always heard that voice within me. I just never acknowledged or recognized it as being from God. He's always been there for me and I am finally starting to give him his due attention.

Certainly our God is very much alive and dramatic healing (also known as miracles) are very possible and do happen. Dramatic healing has also occurred after a very cleansing confession as we make ourselves right with our God and relieve our conscious.

The next three incidents involve the Word of Knowledge given to me on three consecutive days at a seminar I attended that turned out to be related in nature and provided me with an inner healing I was not even aware of.

The prayer teams that assembled in the conference room gave me a Word to forgive my father, which I had done during the course of reading the prayer of forgiveness. But I did go back and forgive him for dying some 27 years ago. I, as the eldest of nine siblings, dropped out of college to help out at home, started working full-time. Later I went back to school full-time nights to finish school for myself, and as a promise I made to my mother.

The next day after the anointing, my back started bothering me as it had been since the beginning of the year. I attributed it to being a catcher for the third night in a row. I approached Bill and asked for prayer, and again, he immediately said I needed to forgive my father! I thought to myself, "How many times do I have to forgive him for the same thing?" But I went into chapel to meditate on the rosary and asked if there was something else I needed to forgive my father for. Barely two minutes into prayer, it hit me. An event that occurred when I was no more that 8- or 10-years-old. My dad was in a room with two others, who had a very noticeable hump on their backs. One of them made a statement that I also was slightly hunched, not knowing that I overheard this in the next room. My Dad, being the nonconfrontational, passive person he was, agreed with them. Ever since then I was determined not to become a hunchback and started sleeping with pillows underneath my shoulder blades, determined to straighten my back out. To this day, I had still maintained that habit even though I had long since forgotten why. But I wasn't going to disappoint my father by growing up with a hump on my back.

Needless to say, a chill went down my back as I recalled this incident and I forgave my father along with all the others who were in the room that day. My back felt better the next day! All I have had since are fond memories of my father and now I will continue to do so.

The younger we are, the more traumatic the impact on our lives. These repressed memories had initially affected me psychologically and a bit emotionally. Later on in life, I started to feel it physically and if that would have continued it may have also impacted me spiritually, as it had in prior relationships. What drives us to react or interact the way we do with the people in our lives. All five of these areas can and are affected by the repressed memories of a traumatic event that occurred in our lives. Most times we are not even aware of the root causes and go through life blaming everyone and everything except the real problem. My meager understanding of this topic cannot begin to do it justice. A good place for anyone to start is John Powell's book referenced in the back.

Believe it or not, the next day during the Word of Knowledge workshop, a word given to me by the man I partnered with was very odd. But as we prayed, yet a third event involving my father surfaced. Who would have thought?

It should not have surprised me how many people went to the seminar searching for ways to help others, not knowing the tremendous healing they themselves would receive. It further reinforced something I heard some time ago, that we are all a hurting, wounded people, despite our appearances.

Conclusion

At a February 2001 retreat, I was feeling a definite blockage to any further release of the Holy Spirit within me so I approached the priest whom had just spoken. I asked him for a quick prayer and a discernment of what may be blocking me, but by now he was so sensitized to the Spirit, he immediately sensed the words within his spirit, "Self-Rage!" I knew I had some work to do in forgiving myself and thought I had done so, but this stunned me for about a minute. Funny though, I had a strange sense of relief because I now knew what I had to deal with and would not dare to question the Holy Spirit who knows me better than I know myself.

The most amazing part of this night though came when I turned to go back to my seat and a big grin soon replaced my prior look of astonishment at the severity of the diagnosis. Sitting right in front of me in this room were over two hundred and fifty prayer warriors, all ready, willing and able and all sensitized to the presence of the Holy Spirit to one degree or another! God wants to pour out his divine love on me so lavishly; he waited to diagnose me in an atmosphere with plenty of back up systems. If any one person were spiritually blocked or unable to help me, I would move on to the next. (Our own Space Shuttle only contains several back up systems) But God was bound and determined to have me leave this place completely healed. As it was, I did indeed require prayer from three different people to help me finally surrender my heart completely, which now belongs to him.

Forgiving and asking forgiveness from others came so effortlessly, so naturally after my born again experience, I couldn't give it or get fast enough from others. Forgiving myself in all the areas I perceived I could have done better or didn't do enough and beating myself up was quite the opposite. I had only superficially forgiven myself prior not knowing the raging battle going on in the cellar of my unconscious mind passively controlling my thoughts and actions, but more importantly, effectively blocking a portion of my heart from being filled with God's love.

Coincidentally, I had received a Word from God several months earlier that said, "Keep giving, but open myself up to receive." Naturally, I interpreted that message to mean open myself up to love from other humans. But I had received such a tremendous healing from the pain and hurt of my prior relationship, I was in no hurry to open myself up that type of misery again.

Now I know I was, in fact, blocking out that portion of my heart from the divine love God was waiting to fill me completely with and really trusting him and knowing he would be with me always.

On the first day of my spiritual awakening, I was almost overwhelmed by the outpouring of love and thought I would explode as his graces were saturating me. That was, however, only filling the portion of my heart that was open to God. I had this secret compartment I was not even aware existed within me that was effectively blocking God from replacing my heart with his.

Right now a double portion of his divine love is saturated into my fully surrendered heart and the feeling is just pure ecstasy!

But that's not the whole story, after prayers with the prayer warriors, at an anointing given by the priest with my eyes closed, a deep shade of blue I had never seen before filled my vision. (I had been told earlier a blue color at this time signified the presence of Mary, the mother of God, just as a deep red color at this time signifies the presence of the Holy Spirit.) I knew Mary was capable of filling us with her motherly love and compassion, but this was different. I felt she had graced me with a touch of the feminine side of her love, something I really needed.

Bottom line is I'm overflowing now with enough love to last me two lifetimes and as a result I'm not afraid to love anymore. "Love others as you love yourself!"

Well, God obviously has a plan for me. I know he has something up his sleeve since he has gone so much out of his way to help me. Even more so than I wanted to help myself, but then again that is his nature to help us Love him as we must first love ourselves before we can love others. Just as it is the nature of birds to fly or fish to swim, the essence of God's nature is LOVE. Now I can really start living life abundantly as it was meant to be, one lived in a relationship with the giver of life. For a God for whom time has no meaning and lives without a clock or calendar, his timing is so perfect.

This same retreat titled, "But if I touched his cloak, I should be cured" had some of the most gifted, intellectuals thinkers of the Catholic Church. As each one spoke, their Words were answers to prayers I have had. A very gifted Fr. Bill McCarthy, gave an unexpected talk on being still and listening to the voice of God within us. Everything I had prayed for and then some as one speaker after the next in one way or another confirmed or affirmed almost everything I have been putting into this document during the past year.

The icing on the cake, however, was when Fr. Robert DeGrandis, the last speaker, challenged us to write out our testimony in seven or eight pages and just start handing it out to everyone we know. Oops, I guess I goofed again, because by now I was at almost forty pages, but I guess that's what confession is for. By the way, is single space and one inch margins O.K. Father?

God is True to his Creation if we remain true to Him.

The Tree

Glories in the Sunshine
Soaks in the Rain
Providing resting place and home to creatures
Place to lean on and rest
Protection from the Sun's Rays
Supplying fruits and nuts for nourishment
Remaining true to it's nature.

The Human Soul

Glories in the Light of the Lord
Soaking in his sweet mercies
Providing a Resting Place and home for his Spirit
Place for others to lean on and rely on
Protection from damaging wind and rain
Supplying Spiritual nourishment
If *only* we could remain true to our nature,
    as God intended us to be.

As every evening arrives and I reflect on all the ways the Lord has used me in that particular day, I give him thanks and praise he thinks so highly of me to use my hands, my feet, my mouth to reach out to others. It is no longer a chore, but a most pleasurable experience. Bill Withers said it best in his popular 70s song: "And if it feels this good being used. Well, then just use me up!"

Even if you remember nothing else of what you have read, please remember in your moment of greatest need, in danger or in great despair, these three little *Powerful* words!

JESUS SAVE ME—It works!

References

God the Father, Son & Holy Spirit

Mary, the Mother of God

Solving the Riddle of Self, John Powell

The Catholic Living Bible

Catholic & Christian, Alan Shreck 1984

The Holy Spirit & You, Dennis & Rita Bennett 1971

Good Morning Holy Spirit, Benny Hinn

When Christ Comes, Max Lucado 1999

What the Bible reveals about Heaven,
    Daniel A. Brown 1999

Pilgrims of Faith, Marion Center

Fr. Robert DeGrandis

Fr. Al Ajamie

Central Indiana Charismatic Association

People of Praise

Power in Praise, Merlin Carothers